First Drawings
CATS

ABDO
Publishing Company

A Buddy Book **by** Marie Hosley

VISIT US AT
www.abdopublishing.com

Published by ABDO Publishing Company, 4940 Viking Drive, Edina, Minnesota 55435.

Copyright © 2007 by Abdo Consulting Group, Inc. International copyrights reserved in all countries. No part of this book may be reproduced in any form without written permission from the publisher. Buddy Books™ is a trademark and logo of ABDO Publishing Company.

Printed in the United States.

Editor: Sarah Tieck
Contributing Editor: Michael P. Goecke
Illustrations: Maria Hosley
Interior Photographs: Photodisc, Photos.com
Interior Photographs: Photos.com, SHdigital

Library of Congress Cataloging-in-Publication Data

Hosley, Maria.
    Cats / Maria Hosley.
       p. cm. — (First drawings)
    Includes index.
    ISBN-13: 978-1-59679-801-4
    ISBN-10: 1-59679-801-7
    1. Cats in art—Juvenile literature. 2. Drawing—Technique—Juvenile literature.
    [1. Cats in art. 2. Drawing—Technique.] I. Title.

NC783.8.C36H67 2007
743.6'9752—dc22
                                                                    2006032078

Table Of Contents

Getting Started

Today you're going to learn to draw a cat. Not sure you know how to draw? If you know how to make circles, squares, and triangles, you can draw most anything!

You will learn to draw in four steps. First, you will measure to get the correct sizes. Next, you will lightly draw the basic shapes. This helps you construct a cat. From those basic shapes, you will make the final outline. And last, you will erase the basic shape lines and add **detail**.

Can you see the basic shapes
in the picture of the real cat?

To draw a cat, you'll need paper, a
sharpened pencil, a big eraser, and a hard,
flat surface. Many artists like to draw at a
table or a desk. They sit up straight with
their tools in front of them. Gather your
supplies. Then, let's get started!

ARTIST'S TOOLBOX

Most cats don't sit still long enough to be **sketched**. So, you may need to find a **reference** picture. Many artists draw from these images. Some have folders filled with them!

Start your own reference folder by collecting photographs or pictures from magazines. Then, use them as you draw. This book has a reference picture of a cat to get you started.

REFERENCE PICTURES

Measurements and Proportions

Have you ever looked at a drawing and thought about whether it looks real? Many people draw cats that look like the real-life animal.

To make a **realistic** drawing of a cat, find out the cat's proportions. Proportion is the size of one thing compared to another. For example, a cat's head should be a size that fits with the rest of its body. Using correct proportions helps make your cat drawing look realistic.

There is an easy way to match the proportions of a real-life cat for your drawing. You can use strips of paper to measure the body parts on your reference picture. Here's how to do it:

Cut a strip of paper the same width as the cat's head. Then, make several more strips of the same size.

Lay the strips on the cat. Do this to compare the head size with the body width and the cat's height.

The body is about 2 strips wide.

The cat's height is a little more than 3 strips.

Choosing A Size For Your Drawing

To draw this cat at this size, cut several strips of paper that match the length of the orange strips shown above.

If you want a larger drawing, cut longer strips. And if you want a smaller drawing, cut shorter strips. Just make sure the strips fit on your drawing paper.

Place your cut strips on your drawing paper. Arrange them so they match the reference picture. With your pencil, lightly mark the ends of each strip.

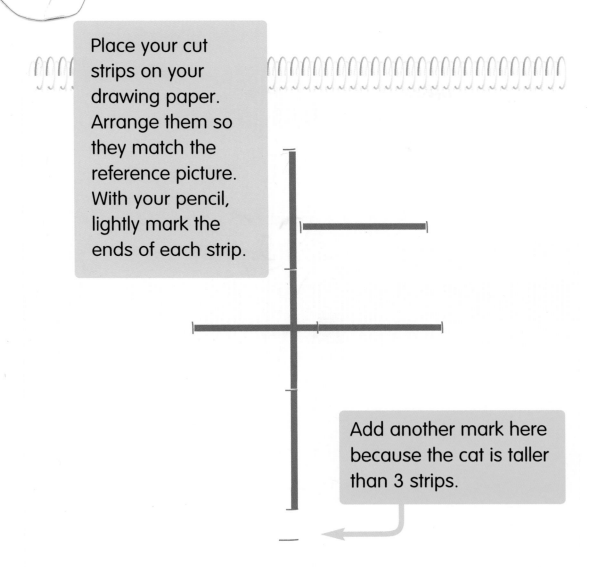

Add another mark here because the cat is taller than 3 strips.

Basic Shapes

All things are easier to draw if you break them down into basic shapes. Draw these shapes *very lightly*. They are only a guide that you will erase later. And when the lines are light, it is easy to erase and try again. Remember to use your proportion lines as a guide!

Between your top guidelines, draw a wide oval for the face. Put in circles for the cheeks. And, add triangles to the top for the ears. Draw tall ovals for the body. Finally, **sketch** lines for the legs and the tail and ovals for the paws.

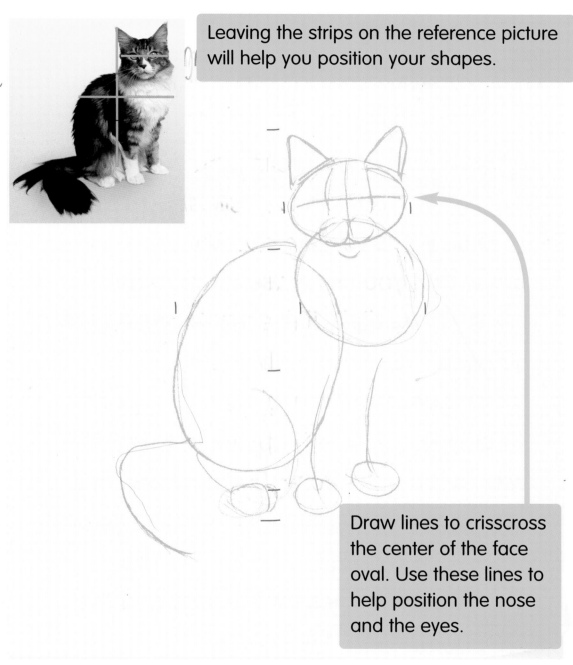

Leaving the strips on the reference picture will help you position your shapes.

Draw lines to crisscross the center of the face oval. Use these lines to help position the nose and the eyes.

Final Outline

Now you have drawn the basic shapes for your cat! You can use them to make the final outline shape. Do this *lightly* with a pencil.

Follow around the outside of the basic shapes to give your cat shape. Draw the legs and the tail. Add lines to shape the eyes, nose, and mouth. Last, put in lines to define the paws.

Adding Detail

Once you are happy with your outline, erase the basic shape lines. Be careful not to erase any lines you still need.

Now you can add the **details**! Along the entire outline, add lines for the cat's hair. Draw longer hairs around the ears. And add whiskers. Then, round and shade the eyes and the nose.

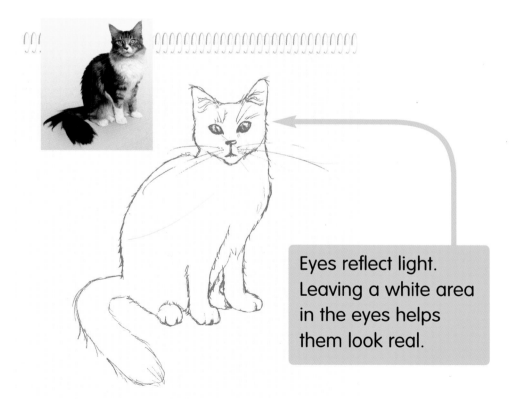

Eyes reflect light. Leaving a white area in the eyes helps them look real.

When you are happy with your outline and **details**, you can make them darker. Do this with your pencil or a marker. Erase any extra lines, and you're done!

Keep Drawing

You have now finished a drawing of a cat. Good job! Use these steps next time you want to draw something.

Don't worry if drawing feels like a challenge at first. Like anything else, drawing takes practice.

Have fun with your new skills. And remember to practice, practice, practice! The more you draw the better you will become.

Want to keep improving your skills? Try using colored pencils to add color to your cat. Add a background to your drawing, too.

Draw your colored pencil lines in the same direction that the cat's hair grows.

Caricature Cats

It is fun to **exaggerate** parts of the cat. This is how you make a caricature. A caricature is a picture that looks like a cartoon.

Choose one body part or feature of the cat. Then, exaggerate it to make it look funny. Just use your imagination!

You can make a cat have human facial **expressions**. Practice drawing cat faces that show emotion. Then, try making your cat's body position match its mood.

SAD

shocked

happy

Using the same basic shapes, we created a caricature of the cat. We made his head larger, gave him a crooked smile, put his paw on cards, and flipped up his tail. These details make him look sly!

Important Words

detail a minor decoration, such as a cat's whiskers.

exaggerate to make something seem larger or different than it really is.

expression a look that shows feeling.

realistic showing things as they are in real life.

reference a picture or an item used for information or help.

sketch to make a rough drawing.

Web Sites

To learn more about drawing cats, visit ABDO Publishing Company on the World Wide Web. Web site links about drawing cats are featured on our Book Links page. These links are routinely monitored and updated to provide the most current information available.

www.abdopublishing.com

Index